FINISHING LINE PRESS

www.finishinglinepress.com

These Domestic Incidences

poems by

Lara Adams Gaydos

Finishing Line Press
Georgetown, Kentucky

These Domestic Incidences

For the Girl and the Boy,
and for Joe. Always.

ACKNOWLEDGMENTS

The author is grateful to Pam Northen, Christine Geller, Danelle Miller, Pam
Smith, Ceil Malek, Liz Lewis, Mimi Wheatwind, Janice Gould, and the late Lois
Beebe Hayna for their excellent insight, critique, and support of the poems in
this book.

This book would not have been possible without the help of Dr. Christopher
Bursk. His many read-throughs of this manuscript, his critical insights of
these poems, both individually and as a whole, and his enduring support and
enthusiasm for this project proved to be invaluable, as always.

Special thanks to Abigail Gaydos, for her exquisite cover art.

And finally, many thanks also go to Christen Kincaid, Leah Maines, and
everyone at Finishing Line Press for all of their hard work, patience, and help.

Publisher: Leah Maines
Editor: Christen Kincaid
Cover Art: Abigail Gaydos
Author Photo: Lara Gaydos
Cover Design: Leah Huete

Printed in the USA on acid-free paper.
Order online: www.finishinglinepress.com
          also available on amazon.com

Author inquiries and mail orders:
Finishing Line Press
P. O. Box 1626
Georgetown, Kentucky 40324
U. S. A.

Table of Contents

Girl Screaming on an Early Summer Night

Last night we heard a girl screaming
faintly through the windows closed
against the evening's summer chill,
her voice young, but insistent enough
to make my teenage daughter and me look
at each other in that certain questioning way—
brow furrowed, head slightly cocked,
the whole body already anticipating
a possible adrenaline rush if this tiny
ambiguous fraction-of-a-heartbeat moment
turns out to be something serious.
When the second shriek came, wordlessly
we both rose from our chairs, went quickly to
the front door to peer out into the dark,

(and, Jesus, this is just how it started last time
except it was Joe standing next to me, not Abby,
and it was October then, not June, and so cold—)

but this time there was nothing to see,
and no more screams after that.
I guess the girl is okay, if it was a girl.
It could have been just an owl,
or even one of the mountain lions
that still prowl through our little piece
of this pine forest at the top of the divide,
along with a remnant pack of coyotes,
the occasional bobcat, black bear.

Every so often, you see in the local news
a troubling story of how someone got too close
to a den, or somehow provoked a lethal predator
you didn't even know lived right here
in this place you thought was so safe
you hardly think twice when your daughter

spends most of her summer evenings outside
swinging on the swing set, until, that is,
you hear her cry out and run for the house.
Wild-eyed, chest heaving, she bursts through
the kitchen door, saying she heard something big
stalking around in the trees behind her.

Life is full of these unexpected frights.
You scream your screams and move on.

In the Days between the Shooting
and the Appointment with the Carpet Guy

A tasteful few days after the shooting, well-meaning
friends begin to stop by to see how you're holding up.
Arriving in groups of two or three, speaking gently,
they cross the damaged threshold and become
inevitably transfixed by the garish thick globs
of dried-on ground-in reddish brown muck
that coats what's left of your plush cream carpeting.
They take mincing steps, not wanting to touch
any of it, ask in hesitant tones: "Is that…?"

Most of them bring along a small edible offering:
a banana bread, or a plate of store-bought cookies,
something that pairs well with coffee. No
dinners or casseroles. Just desserts. After all,
no one actually died in your house. Not like
up on the corner where the real action happened.
That house is empty now, still crisscrossed
with yellow crime-scene tape. The neighborhood
kids stroll by, linger out front as if working on
the final drafts of their ghost stories:
They say the mother is still in there, guarding
the closet where her youngest daughter hid….
All the local sleepovers now include a tour of
the street where the shooting happened,
a journey that ends in front of your house, where
you're standing in the dining room holding a plate
of something sweet, patiently explaining once more,

"No, that's not blood. That's mud.
It was muddy that night and the police
and firemen tracked it all over the place."
"Oh," your guests say, in a quiet, funny way,
making you wonder: are they relieved,
or disappointed? Just in case it's the latter,

you take them on your own little tour
through your living room and study,
lifting up large, strategically placed floor baskets
full of cat toys, yarn, and magazines to reveal
the gaping rectangular holes in your carpet,
and you say, "They cut out all the blood-
stained areas and took them away. As evidence."
Then you all go back to the dining room to eat cake.

Please Let Me In, She Says

Some days, I lose it a little, like this morning, when
the girls misplaced their piano books (again),
and it occurred to me that maybe
they hadn't been practicing their lessons (again).
I lecture them in the car all the way to town:
how I already had two jobs by the time I was their age,
how much piano books cost, how good they've got it
compared to most of the children in this world.
I'm remembering the night of the shooting, of course,
but my daughters don't know that story yet,
and today is not the right day to tell them.

Even after all these years, I can still see the girl
coming up my front steps in the night:
hunched over, staggering to the door,
where I've been peering out the side-light window,
having heard some screams. She sags against
the other side of the glass, sobbing,
her face pale, her dark eyes panicked.
"Please let me in," she says. "My dad shot me."
Joe hears the commotion and joins me at the door.
"What is it?" he asks. I look at him numbly.
"It's a girl. She says she's been shot."
We stare at each other a moment more,
and then we're both reaching for the knob.
It's the only part of the night that happens slowly.
We open the door wide and she stumbles in,
collapses right there in the foyer.
A blast of frigid air blows in with her.
As I move to shut the door against the wind
I see another child running up the porch steps:
a small boy, shirtless and barefoot.
He rushes through the entryway, falls to the floor
next to the girl and says, "Call 911."

Today, nearly twenty years later, I catch a glimpse
of my daughters in the rearview mirror as we speed
south on the Interstate toward the Conservatory,
both of them staring pointedly out the windows
as I continue to hold relentlessly forth on the value
of piano lessons, the commitment to practice,
the ease of our fortunate lives, while in my mind,
the girl and her brother keel over in my front hall
again and again, and I find myself wishing
I could claw my way out of both that memory
and this brief moment of parental failure in my car.

**"Wounded Kids Ran to Neighbor;
Bloody Clothes Mistaken for Halloween Costumes"**

—Headline from the Rocky Mountain News, Oct. 28, 1996, p.4A

Joe's already dialing 911 while I stare down
at these two children lying prone on my foyer floor.
It's only a few days until Halloween and a little part
of me is waiting for them to leap up and holler
"FOOLED YA!!" And that little part of me
is already working on the furious lecture
I will deliver unto them for scaring me like this.

But they're not getting up, dammit.
The girl is curled in a fetal comma,
her arms cradling her abdomen,
moaning, "it hurts, it hurts…"
and the shirtless boy lies face down,
a small bullet hole in his back, high up,
ominously close to his spine.
Blood trickles delicately from it,
tracing a thin red line to his waist.

Get up! I want to shout. *Stop this!*
Instead I say, "Who did this to you?"
"My dad," the girl sobs.
I peer through the side-light window at the street,
the paved walk leading up to my steps,
everything quiet but alarmingly well-lit,
and ask, "Where is your father right now?"
"I don't know," the girls cries.
The boy says nothing at all. I reach
a hand out, shut off the porch and foyer lights.

I dart around the house, turning off more lights,
drawing blinds and curtains. When all is dark,
I return to the kids. "We have to move. Right now."
"I can't," the girl says, crying harder.
"Yes, you can," I say. "I'll help you.
Just down the hall a bit. Away from this window."
Her brother is already on his feet.
He follows me as I half-drag the girl
across the living room and into my study,
its lone window higher up and already shaded,
and the two of them collapse once more.

In an hour or so, I'll be seated on the sofa
at my next door neighbor's house, shakily
telling her how at first I kept thinking
they were just playing a Halloween prank.
I'll get stuck on that for a while.
My neighbor will pat my hand, freshen my tea,
tell me not to worry about it. Then
she'll share this tidbit with a reporter
the very next day, while Joe and I are out
having lunch and buying a gun,
and the day after that I'll open the paper,
read all about the things I thought.

That's What You Do, Right?

The boy lay on his belly: silent, pale,
staring blankly off into space, probably in shock,
certainly freezing after running up the street
half-clad in the unexpected cold. The girl
was better dressed for this sort of thing
in dark gray sweats conveniently soaking up
most of the blood leaking from her abdomen.
My mind dredged up some old first aid
advice about keeping shock victims warm,
so I covered them with blankets—just a couple
of decorative throws I kept handy in the living room.

But then I wondered, should I apply pressure
to their wounds? That's what you do
when someone's bleeding, right?
I ran to the kitchen for some dishtowels.
Back in the study, I pulled the blankets off the kids,
then froze, unable to decide who was hurt worse.
I tried lifting up the girl's sweatshirt to see
her wound, but the dim light only revealed
a dark bloody smear. And the hole in the boy's back
was so close to his spine I was afraid to touch it,
afraid I'd push the bullet even closer to his spine.

They had landed some distance from each other
on the study floor. To be effective at all,
I'd have to choose one over the other.
Instead, I knelt between them, my arms
stretched wide, just able to reach them both,
and rested the dishtowels lightly on their bodies,
the blankets puddled and forgotten at their feet.

After a while, I started to pray. That's what you do
when something like this happens. Right?

Joe on the Phone with 911

He calls from the kitchen wall phone,
inadvertently tethering himself to that location
while I move frantically about. He says
we need an ambulance, and the police.
He says please hurry, two children have been shot.
They keep him on the phone the whole time.

They ask so many questions.
They ask our names, our ages, our address.
They ask the children's names, and their ages.
They ask where the children's injuries are.
They ask if Joe is injured. If I am injured.
They ask if these are our children.
Then they ask how we know these children.

They ask if we have any guns in the house.
They ask if the shooter is inside the house.
They ask if we know who the shooter is.
They ask if we know *where* the shooter is.
They say help is on the way.
They don't let him hang up.

Big Bad Wolf

Not by the hair of my chinny-chin-chin.
—Joseph Jacobs, The Three Little Pigs

There was some talk between us
in that endless twenty minutes
the three of us spent together
in the darkened little study
of my sturdy little house.
Most of that talk is lost to me now,
except for the part where I said to them:

I need you both to be as quiet as you can,
but you can't go to sleep. Okay?

That part I remember quite well.
Because we were hiding, you see.

We were hiding from their father,
who might have been stalking
up the street (huffing and puffing)
looking for them even as we whispered
little essential things to each other.
Things like:

It hurts, it hurts.
I know, honey. It's going to be okay.
I'm afraid.
I know, honey. I'm here.
I don't want to die.
You won't, honey. I promise.

And then,
when the knocking at the door started:
Shhhhhhh....

Waiting, Whispering, Listening

…shortly after the neighbors took the children in, a man came
pounding at their front door. They believed it was the shooter.
"That's not totally unreasonable speculation," Aurora police said.
"We're not sure, but it could have been him."
—Rocky Mountain News, 10-28-96, p.4A

Joe, scrunched down under the kitchen window,
making himself small in the dark, whispers to 911,
"Someone's knocking at the door. Is it the police?"

The dispatcher says, "Sir, at this time, we cannot confirm
that it's the police. Do not open your door."
The knocking stops abruptly, but starts again

a minute later, on the dining room slider. Joe says,
"Now they're at the side door. Is it the police?"
The dispatcher says, "No sir. We still cannot confirm.

Do not open your door." The knocking stops again,
and we hear a faint crunch of footsteps on gravel.
"He's circling the house," Joe whispers.

"Sir, do not open your door. Stay on the line."
For an eternal while, all the world is this
knock-knock-knock, crunch-crunch-crunch

of a stranger trying to get inside, and Joe
asking 911,"what do I do if he gets in?"
again and again, while across the hall

on the study floor, I reach for the children's hands,
squeeze gently, breathe out one more shush
and then hold what little air I've got left,

as I tilt my head toward the study window,
listening as those footsteps come to a halt
just on the other side of the shade.

Perspective

What I was thinking in the dark,
waiting for the police to come,
hunched over two bleeding children,
someone trying to break into the house:
If he gets in here, we're dead.

What Joe was thinking in the dark,
crouched low under the kitchen window,
stuck on the phone with 911,
an unknown assailant hammering at the door:
If he gets in here, how can I take him down?

Joe in the kitchen; me in my study.
Not much square footage between us
in that little starter house of ours,
just a dining room and a hallway, really.
But perspective is a tricky thing,
making the distance between us,
in that brief moment, unfathomable.

Argument

"Go to the basement," Joe said. "Right now!"
"I can't get them down those stairs!" I snarled.
"You have to leave the kids."
"What? No!"
"You have to. That's what they said.
You have to hide. You can't help them
if you get shot. So go downstairs.
Right now. Hurry, dammit!

He was beginning to yammer,
to panic, and I understood
what he was saying,
what *they* were saying.
So I went.
Had I known how many times
detectives, counselors,
even the shooter's lawyer,
would ask in delicate,
narrow tones, why I left the children,
maybe I would have stayed.

Report from Under the Basement Stairs

Everything echoes down here in the pitch dark,
all sounds amplified a dozen-fold:
the knocking at the front door
now a hammering full-on assault,
Joe's voice, garbled but louder,
still on the phone with 911,
the girl's sobs right above my head.

Then footsteps crossing the living room floor,
and Joe's voice again, a clear shout:
It's jammed! Go around to the side!
More footsteps, moving faster
to the patio door in the dining room.
And then a veritable stampede of heavy
authoritative feet pouring inside,
the girl calling out, *help me! help me!*

Cavalry

At last the basement door opens.
A voice calls: is there anyone down there?

Upstairs, everything now a crowded confusion
of strobing flashlights, armed men talking over each other,

the bloody children in my study surrounded by
so many medics, you can't see them at all.

An officer asks if I am injured. I say no.
He points to the side door and orders me outside.

As I step over the threshold into the frigid air,
a helicopter lands in my front yard.

The roar and chop of its rotor blades almost drowns out
the shouts of more police officers running around,

barking importantly into radios, putting up yellow tape,
all of them awash in flashes of red and blue light.

I raise a hand against the helicopter's glare and see
Joe, kneeling in the half-frozen mud, handcuffed,

a cop behind him, gun drawn and held on him,
and I have a torrent of furious words to say about that,

but Joe is calm, Joe is steady, Joe is not moving
a muscle. *I'm okay,* he says. *It's all right.*

The cop outside orders me back inside.
I tell him the cop inside just ordered me outside,

so the cop brings us both back inside, makes us
sit on the kitchen floor, disappears into the fray.

We huddle together in the pandemonium
that is known as 'securing the scene.'

Name, Age, Date of Birth

Back outside again. I have my coat on now,
a fresh pack of Marlboros in my pocket,
a lit cigarette tucked between my fingers.
Another cop is asking me my name and birthdate.
Half a dozen of his colleagues have already asked
these questions, written the answers down
in very important looking notepads,
told me to stay put, and then wandered off.
This cop is different, though. This one asks,
"…and how old are your children?"
I shake my head a little, blow smoke politely
past his shoulder, and say, "They're not ours."
He stares at me blankly, so I continue impatiently,
"We don't have any children. I don't know
who they are or where they came from.
They probably live somewhere nearby."
When he finally gets it, you can almost hear the click.
"Stay right here," he says, already turning away,
reaching for his radio. An anxious cloud of cops
forms around him at the end of the driveway.
I'm shivering. I tell myself it's only because of the cold.

And Suddenly, There Were Teenagers Everywhere

They arrive in a fluttery swarm, like moths
attracted to the unrelenting strobes of red and blue,
and the bright lights of the helicopter taking off,
airlifting those bullet-ridden children to a hospital.
I'm standing on the sidewalk, smoking,
watching yellow tape go up around my house,
when the startling noise of them washes over me.
The teens laugh and scream, jump up and down,
rub their bare tattooed arms against the cold,
run from lawn to lawn, as if trying to find
the center of all this suburban excitement.
Without the helicopter, it's not as clear anymore.

Disoriented, they knock into each other, struggle
like a line of ants when you sweep up the sugar spill
they'd just been plundering and throw it away.
I drag deeply on my cigarette, my lungs burn
a little from the smoke plus the biting air.
When I exhale, I breathe extra hard but still
I can't tell when the smoke ends and vapor begins.
Suddenly out of the dark, a boy rushes at me,
breathless, grinning, his eyes gleaming.
"So… what *happened*?" he asks, bouncing on his toes.
I look around for a cop, but there aren't any near,
so after a moment's stare, I reply, "You know…
I don't think I'm supposed to talk to you."
His smile never falters. "That's okay," he says.
"That's cool, man." He trots away
down the sidewalk, back into the street.
The others flock, grackle-like, toward him.
For a brief while, he is the focal point of the night.

Capture

"Is that [expletive] dead?"
[the boy] asked a police officer....
"You kill that [expletive]?"
　　　　—*Rocky Mountain News, 11-14-96, p.4A*

The police find him in his own home,
just five doors up, on the corner.
He's sitting on his bed nursing
a bullet wound in his shoulder,
his wife dead at his feet.

He claims his wife shot him first,
that everything that followed
was self-defense, but forensics
and the testimony of the girl
and the boy will prove him a liar.

They search the house and find
a six-year-old girl tucked deep
in a closet. They coax her out.
She says her brother and sister
hid her in there before they left.
Her stepfather had taken a shot
at her earlier, but missed.

There will be no trial.
He pleads guilty to a lesser charge.
Our testimony is conducted
completely over the phone.
We never have to go to court.
We see his face only in the paper,
only if we choose to open it.

Neighborly

We're told we can't enter our house
until the investigation is complete.
We're also told we can't leave the area, so
our next door neighbors—a young man
and his elderly mother—take us in for the night.
An officer is stationed inside the front door
to keep reporters and gawkers at bay.
It's the same cop who had a gun on Joe earlier.
He keeps apologizing for this; we keep
forgiving him. The 10:00 news is on
and getting it all wrong. Someone makes tea.
We wait there for the detectives to come.

They interview us separately. My detective
looks and sounds exactly like Sam Elliott.
We go through it slowly. I can't remember
what the kids' faces looked like or the color
of the girl's sweat suit. But the boy's bare back,
the small entry wound with its trail of blood,
his dark eyes clouded with shock,
the girl crying, collapsing and writhing
on my floor, all that will stay with me.

Our neighbors make up the sofa bed for us.
From their kitchen window, I can see across
into my own dining room, still a flurry
of activity over there, men milling about
with clipboards and tape measures,
every seat at the table taken up by officers
filling out paperwork, talking on radios
or telephones, sipping from Styrofoam cups.

We settle in for the night, the TV
still on, the news mercifully over,
some sit-com or other coming to an end.
The screen goes dark for a moment,
then a disembodied voice announces the beginning
of daylight savings time and sets the clock
back one hour. Next, with a heraldry of trumpets
and electric guitars, comes an old episode
of *CHiP's*. We watch the opening credits,
as Ponch and Jon zip around on their motorcyles,
dodging bullets, bad guys, and explosions,
and pretty soon we're both laughing uncontrollably.
We stuff our faces into our pillows,
try to chuff it out as quietly as possible.
What will the neighbors think?

The Boy in the Hospital

The surgery to remove the bullet
lodged next to his spine went well,
and now he's settled into the PICU
where he'll remain for several days.
He wakes in the night,
restless and alone, groggy
from the pain medication.
He turns on the TV just in time
to see two uniformed men
carrying a large, plastic body-bag
out his own front door.
That's how he finds out
his mother didn't make it.

The Girl in the Hospital

Every time the news comes on,
the girl looks for me.
We're still the top story,
will be for most of the week,
and the entire neighborhood
(except for us)
has taken their turn
in front of the cameras.

Whenever she sees
a woman being interviewed,
the girl becomes agitated,
asking, "Is that her? Is that her?"
over and over again.
She can remember my face
about as well as I can remember hers.

"No, sweetie, that's not her,"
her aunt keeps saying.
"They haven't been on TV at all."
She strokes the girl's long sable hair
intently, smoothing it back from
that young, fretful brow,
saves her own tears for later.

This Particular Madness

Reporters come calling, ringing the bell
relentlessly for days on end, sliding business cards
under the door, private numbers scribbled on the backs.
I hide in the bedroom when they knock,
while Joe patiently, pleasantly, turns them away.
He's better at this that I ever could be.

On the news, medics carry a body bag
out of the house on the corner. A camera
traces the route the kids took to our house.
Little drops of blood on the sidewalk
lead the way, breadcrumb-like, down the street,
then up my porch steps to my front door,
battered and dented where the cops tried to kick it in.
This becomes our story's signature footage,
looping endlessly on the screen while
neighbor after neighbor after neighbor
steps up to the microphone. They all say
the same thing: they're just shocked
something like this could happen here.

They keep the reporters mercifully busy
that first week. Soon we drop from the lead story
to the second, to the third, to the weekly update,
and finally to just a blip in News 9's year-in-review.
We manage to avoid this particular madness
with surprising ease; our names and faces
never do appear in print or on the air.
In a couple of months, all those news vans
would move on to a far juicier story:
a dead little white girl, beauty queen
from the wealthier side of town, strangled
in her own basement on Christmas Eve.
They're still trying to figure that one out.

Thank You

She telephones first, on the evening after,
and deft as he is at warding off reporters,
this is a call Joe cannot take. "It's their aunt," he says,
helplessly handing the receiver over to me.
I hold it to my chest and ask, "What's wrong?"
"She shouldn't have to thank us," he says.
"No," I tell him. "You don't understand.
This is part of it. We have to let her say it."

I put the phone to my ear, settle into a chair
amid the mess: dishes still unwashed, dining table
strewn with discarded forms, crumpled napkins,
coffee cups with cold dregs congealing at the bottom,
the carpet reduced to a muddy, cut-up ruin.
The woman's voice is quiet and breathy.
She tells me the girl and the boy will recover.
She says thank you. She keeps interrupting
herself to say it again and again. I let her
ramble on, punctuating her words with
the usual little niceties: you're welcome,
it was nothing, we did what anyone would do.

A few days later, she and her husband come to visit.
We sit in an awkward silence while coffee brews.
She eyes the ruined carpet, caked thick
with mud and dried clay. "My goodness," she says,
"they must have really run around in here,"
her tone alarmed, apologetic, as if she
had just discovered her children had been
fighting in church or talking back to a teacher.
"Oh, no," I assure her. "The kids didn't do that.
The rescue people tracked all that in."
She looks pointedly at me, and I smile.
"They were very well behaved," I say.

The Waiting Room at Victims Counseling Services

The counselor emerges from her office
to greet us, warm smile, hand held out,
seemingly harmless, but
the first thing she says is,
"So, you're the heroes!"
her voice trumpet-like, her grin
stretching distrustfully wider.
I lean backward, away from her
even as I grasp her hand, murmuring
"I don't know about that,"
while in my mind

I see myself disappear
down those basement stairs again.
I'll be right back, was the last thing I said
to the two of them that night,
and that was nothing but a lie, and now

I suspect the counselor is testing us
with this statement, that later on
after we're gone, she'll write self-important
therapeutic notes on how we reacted
to the word *heroes*, a useless little word
no one else has bothered with.

In the End, It's Roger Who Saves the Hero's Soul

There are flowers on my desk
the day I return to work,
encouraging little greeting cards
propped against my computer monitor,
a concerned message from the CEO
waiting for me in my voice mail box.

Co-workers say good morning,
but then hang back, unsure,
until Roger comes out of his office,
peeks his head around my cubicle
and asks, "Are you all right?"

Before I know it, I'm spilling
the whole story, first just to Roger,
who leans against the countertop
and listens, but then to others
who quietly roll their chairs in
and sit with me as I leech this thing out.

When I get to the part where
I left the children and went to the basement,
my voice hitches and I have to stop.
The entire group makes this subtle noise,
this collective little gasping, **oh….**

Roger leans toward me, takes my hand.
"You did the right thing," he says,
and everyone else nods sensibly.
"I guess so," I say, with a whispery sigh.
Roger shakes his head almost sternly at me.
He squeezes my hand tightly, says it again.

Wish a Poet's Wish

"A postal worker allegedly killed his wife and tried to kill three step-children because one child left a cordless phone in the wrong room...."
  —*Rocky Mountain News*, 11-14-96, p.4A

Nineteen years down our own particular road,
Joe and I sit together at our kitchen table,
a bit grayer and wider now, maybe a bit wiser.
Our two teenaged daughters, only a few years older
than the girl and the boy were that long ago
frosty October night, flit in and out
of the room, leaving a comfortable detritus
in their wake as they dally and bicker
through this lazy summer afternoon:
apple cores, cheese stick and protein bar wrappers,
cast-off sneakers, socks, flip-flops,
forgotten headphones, dog-eared paperbacks,
cell phones and iPods in need of charging,
things I've implored them to either throw away
or put away more times than I can count.

Joe lowers the thin sheaf of papers he's been reading,
the first draft of these poems. He breathes deeply, says,
"That knocking. Think it was the cops the whole time?"
"Probably," I say. We smile ruefully at each other.
"How old do you think they are now?" he asks.
"About 30," I say. "Older than we were that night."
Joe taps the papers on the table to straighten them.
"How do you remember all this stuff?" he asks.
All I can do is smile again, shake my head,
shrug a poet's shrug, wish a poet's wish:
Please, somebody, teach me how to forget.

The Second and Third Things

You hear that signature sound, that particular hollow punch, almost gunshot-like, of metal striking metal, a split second before your entire body lurches forward, your head first snapping down, then back into the headrest so fast that your smart velvet headband flies off, lands on the passenger side floor, where you'll find it hours later, after wondering why your hair keeps falling into your eyes when you finally make it to the office, try to get some actual work done, to be a normal person who does normal things, the person you used to be before the shooting. You want to tell your boss you're not someone who is always having something happen to them, but you can't because you have to call a bunch of people to report the guy that rear-ended you on the Interstate during the morning rush.

You managed to steer the car onto an exit ramp without hitting anyone else, and the guy, just a kid, really, in a red pickup, followed you off the highway, hurried to your window, already apologizing. *Are you hurt?* he asked, and then, even worse, he said, *We have to call the police.* But you just couldn't face that, more interviews with more cops. Hell, you'd have probably recognized whoever showed up, so instead you said no, you have to get to work, you're already late, and you're fine, really. You exchanged necessary information and drove away, still shaking. (Your insurance agent will gently chastise you for this later, will tell you you're not supposed to do that, you should have called the police, but you no longer give a damn.) You end up at the doctor's that evening, your neck a strangely loose mess, your back twisted and tight.

The next evening, while you're resting on the sofa, the scent of new carpet still in the air, your husband will suddenly, sharply ask: *What the hell is THAT?* and you'll look down at the floor to see this enormous black spider, shiny and grotesque, creeping elegantly across the new gray plush, and you'll know without even flipping it over to look for the red hour glass on its plump, quarter-sized belly, that it's poison.

Your husband captures it by the leg with some tweezers and you both watch it twist and scramble as he holds it over the kitchen sink, the red mark perfectly, horrifically defined, before he drops it into the disposal and grinds it up. After it's dead, you go into your little study to light a cigarette, hunch miserably in your desk chair, rocking back and forth a bit, trying not to think too much about anything. Your husband comes in, kneels down in front of you like he's going to propose again. He takes your hand and says, "Do you want to move?"

These Domestic Incidences

My detective, the one who reminds me
of Sam Elliott, stops by just after Thanksgiving
to return my dishtowels and blankets,
carefully folded, still encased in evidence bags.

He declines a cup of coffee,
admires the new gray carpeting.
He lingers on the front porch,
his narrow eyes scanning the street,
stopping briefly on the 'for sale' sign
posted at the edge of my lawn,
but all he says is that he hopes we'll stay,
that this really is a safe neighborhood,
these domestic incidences
can happen anywhere.
He tips his hat to me with a smile,
and trots down the steps to his car.
I watch him drive away, my arms
crossed against the chilly air.

Back in the house, I open the evidence bags.
The dishtowels go right in the trash,
but the blankets look salvageable,
with barely any traces of blood,
so I toss them into the wash on a cold soak,
add extra detergent just in case.

Children at the Door Again

They're struggling once more as they approach
my front porch, but this time it's just an argument
over who gets to carry the gift, a fair-sized box
painstakingly wrapped in bright Christmas paper.
In the end, the boy and the youngest sister
each hold one side, while the eldest girl
walks solemnly in front, leading the procession.
She rings the bell and when I open the door,
she smiles and says, "Do you know who I am?"
"Of course I do," I say, opening the door wider.
They shuffle awkwardly over the threshold.
I look further down the street and see their aunt
hurrying toward us, waving. She catches up
just as Joe comes in from the garage.

We open the package carefully
and discover a jelly bean machine,
ornate, old-fashioned, red metal,
complete with a large bag of candy
which we load into the glass top right away.
Joe digs into his pocket for some loose change
and we all choose pennies from his palm.
Each of us takes a turn feeding coins
into the metal slot, turning the wheel,
cupping our hands under the little trap door.
We sit on the floor near the Christmas tree
in a puddle of mild mid-December sunshine
and eat gourmet jelly beans together.

The older two want to see everything,
to show their sister, so we go into the study
and I point to where they both had lain that night.
I'm grateful for the new carpet, that they won't have to
see the mud, or the cut away parts where they bled.
They're both so much taller today
than I remember, with color in their faces,
laughter in their voices. Now all three
move at the speed of rough and tumble,
chasing each other in and out of the house,
screaming the good kind of screams,
the kind you don't have to worry about,
the kind you could listen to all day.

Exit, Stage West

We leave just before dawn,
the eastern horizon a pale pink tinge
out my window. We head north,
up the Interstate, bouncing along
in the cab of a Ryder truck,
the coffees we stopped for
still too hot to sip,
the cat snoozing comfortably
in her carrier under my feet.
Just as the sun rises, we cross
into Wyoming and turn west.
When we get to Salt Lake City,
we'll stop for the night,
order some takeout, listen
to unfamiliar newscasters
tell unfamiliar stories on TV.

We'll reach California late the next day
and before we start our new jobs,
we'll take some time to bask
in the salty January sunshine,
wander the Pacific coastline together,
watching the surfers paddle out
to that certain sweet spot, where
they sit balanced on their boards,
scanning the open water behind them,
patient, hopeful, seeking that telling swell,
subtle at first, but full of possibility.

Lara Adams Gaydos was born and raised in central and northern New Jersey. She graduated from Rutgers University in 1994, and since that time, has split her time living in either Colorado or Pennsylvania. She currently lives in Monument, Colorado with her husband and two daughters, and their several rescued pets.

While in Colorado, she has been an active member of Poetry West, a local poetry society, and while in Pennsylvania, she was named the Bucks County Poet Laureate in 2012. Her poetry has been nominated for a Pushcart Prize and has appeared in several journals and anthologies including *U.S. 1 Worksheets, Slant, the Schuylkill Valley Journal*, and *Poems from the Baca Grande*. Her first chapbook, *Things That Were Only Briefly the Truth*, was published by Finishing Line Press in 2014.